VIRGINIA LOH-HAGAN

BLACK

HOLES

45TH PARALLEL PRESS

Published in the United States of America
by Cherry Lake Publishing
Ann Arbor, Michigan
www.cherrylakepublishing.com

Reading Adviser: Marla Conn, MS, Ed.,
  Literacy specialist, Read-Ability, Inc.
Book Designer: Jessica Rogner

Photo Credits: © Color4260/Shutterstock, cover, 1; © Coconino National
  Forest/Flickr, 5; © NASA/CXC/M.Weiss/WikiMedia/Public Domain, 7;
  © NASA Goddard/NASA ID: GSFC_20171208_Archive_e000386, 8; © NASA
  Goddard/NASA ID: GSFC_20171208_Archive_e001981, 11; © NASA Goddard/
  NASA ID: GSFC_20171208_Archive_e000719, 12; © Vadim Sadovski/
  Shutterstock, 15; © Fer Gregory/Shutterstock, 16; © NASA/NASA ID:
  0700065, 19; © MarcelClemens/Shutterstock, 21; © NASA Goddard/NASA
  ID: GSFC_20171208_Archive_e000608, 23; © NASA/JPL-Caltech, IPAC/
  NASA ID: PIA23005, 25; © Courtesy AIP Emilio Segr`e Visual Archives/
  WikiMedia/Public Domain, 27; © NASA/Jim Grossmann/NASA
  ID: KSC-2012-4073, 29
Graphic Element Credits: © Trigubova Irina/Shutterstock

45th Parallel Press is an imprint of
Cherry Lake Publishing Group

Library of Congress Cataloging-in-Publication Data

Names: Loh-Hagan, Virginia, author. | Loh-Hagan, Virginia.
  Out of this world.
Title: Black holes / by Virginia Loh-Hagan.
Description: Ann Arbor, Michigan : Cherry Lake Publishing, 2020 |
  Series: Out of this world | Includes bibliographical references
  and index.
Identifiers: LCCN 2020006879 (print) | LCCN 2020006880 (ebook) |
  ISBN 9781534169272 (hardcover) | ISBN 9781534170957 (paperback) |
  ISBN 9781534172791 (pdf) | ISBN 9781534174634 (ebook)
Subjects: LCSH: Black holes (Astronomy)-Juvenile literature.
Classification: LCC QB843.B55 L65 2020 (print) | LCC QB843.B55 (ebook) |
  DDC 523.8/875-dc23
LC record available at https://lccn.loc.gov/2020006879
LC ebook record available at https://lccn.loc.gov/2020006880

Printed in the United States of America | Corporate Graphics

TABLE OF CONTENTS

4 . . . . **INTRODUCTION**
What Is the Universe?

6 . . . . **CHAPTER ONE**
What Are Black Holes?

10 . . . . **CHAPTER TWO**
What Are the Types of Black Holes?

14 . . . . **CHAPTER THREE**
What Do Black Holes Do?

18 . . . . **CHAPTER FOUR**
Are Black Holes Dangerous?

22 . . . . **CHAPTER FIVE**
Do Black Holes Die?

26 . . . . **CHAPTER SIX**
Who First Studied Black Holes?

30 . . . . **GLOSSARY**

31 . . . . **FAR-OUT FACTS / LEARN MORE**

32 . . . . **INDEX / ABOUT THE AUTHOR**

WHAT IS THE UNIVERSE?

The universe is huge. It's everything that exists. This includes planets, stars, and outer space. It includes living things on Earth.

The universe contains billions of galaxies. Galaxies are huge space collections. Galaxies are made up of billions of stars, gas, and dust. Galaxies include **solar** systems. Solar means sun. Earth is in the Milky Way galaxy. Galaxies spin in space. They spin very fast. There's a lot of space between stars and galaxies. This space is filled with dust, light, heat, and rays.

Before the birth of the universe, there was no time, space, or matter. Anything that takes up space is matter. Matter can exist in different states. The common states include solid, liquid, and gas. This is why things like air and smoke are considered matter. But the heat and light from a fire aren't matter. These don't take up space.

The universe hasn't always been the same size. It also hasn't always existed. Some scientists believe it began with a "big bang."

 The Milky Way has about 100 to 400 billion stars.

This is a **theory**. Theory means an idea. This theory explains how the universe was born. First, the universe was a super tiny blob, smaller than a pinhead! Then, that super tiny blob exploded. This happened 13.8 billion years ago. Next, energy spread out. Energy is made from matter. For example, the flames in a fire are matter. They take up space. But the heat you feel and the light you see from the flames are energy. Last, stars and planets formed. This all happened in less than a second.

Scientists think the universe is still expanding. Expanding means growing or spreading out. Scientists also think this expanding process is speeding up.

CHAPTER → ONE

WHAT ARE BLACK HOLES?

Black holes are **dense** areas in space. Dense means crowded and solid. Black holes make deep **gravity** drains. Gravity is a force that pulls things toward Earth's center. It's why things don't float away. It's why things fall down. The deeper the gravity sinks, the more space distorts and curves. Distort means to change out of shape.

Black holes have strong gravity. They have a strong pull. They force things to fall into them. They pull so much that nothing escapes. Light can't even escape. This means black holes can't be seen. It's why they're black.

The first black hole to be "seen" is Cygnus X-1.

To study them, scientists use special space telescopes. Telescopes are used to see faraway objects. Scientists study how stars act.

Stars near black holes act differently from other stars. Black holes pull in dust and gases from nearby stars. The dust and gases heat up. They speed up. They get brighter. The stars near black holes give off high-energy rays. They do this right before going into black holes. Scientists can see these rays.

The boundary of black holes is called the "event horizon." This is the point of no return. Matter can get in. But it can't get out. Scientists have no idea what's happening in there. No signals come from the inside. The gravity is strong because matter has been squeezed into a tiny space. This can happen when stars die.

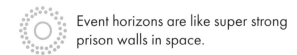

Event horizons are like super strong prison walls in space.

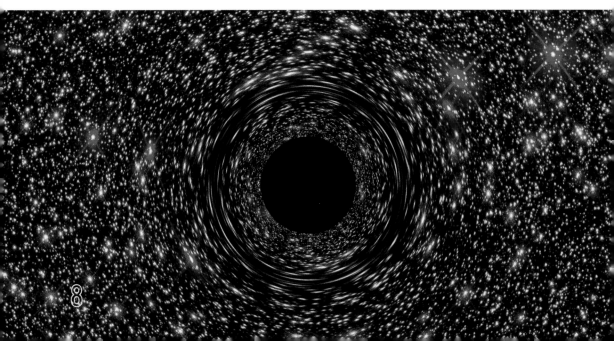

AMONG THE STARS: WOMEN IN SCIENCE

Dr. Katie Bouman was born around 1990. She grew up in Indiana. She's an American computer scientist. She studied electrical engineering. She got degrees from the University of Michigan and Massachusetts Institute of Technology. She teaches at California Institute of Technology. She was a member of the Event Horizon Telescope in 2013. This telescope is a network of 8 telescopes. These telescopes are all over the world. Bouman helped to connect all the data from the different telescopes. She turned a lot of data into a picture. She worked on the code for 3 years. The Event Horizon Telescope took the first photograph of a black hole. The supermassive black hole is in the Messier 87 galaxy. Supermassive means really big. She said, "No one algorithm or person made this image ... I'd like to encourage all of you to go out and help push the boundaries of science, even if it may at first seem as mysterious to you as a black hole."

CHAPTER TWO

WHAT ARE THE TYPES OF BLACK HOLES?

Black holes can be big or small. They grow in size by taking in galaxy matter. They're sorted by **mass**. Mass is the amount of matter in an object. There are 4 main types of black holes.

Primordial black holes formed after the big bang. Primordial means existing at the beginning of time. They're the smallest black holes. They're tiny. But they have the mass of big mountains.

Stellar black holes have 20 times more mass than the Sun. They are the most common. Stellar means stars. When stars can't make energy, they explode. The remaining core closes in. It forms a dense area. This is due to gravity. The density becomes stellar black holes.

Intermediate black holes have masses equal to thousands of suns. Intermediate means coming between 2 things. The amount of mass in an intermediate black hole is between the amounts in stellar and supermassive black holes.

 The Milky Way has 10 million to 1 billion stellar black holes.

Supermassive black holes are the largest. Their masses are equal to millions of suns. They may have been formed when star clusters collapsed together. Every large galaxy has a supermassive black hole at its center. Supermassive black holes were made at the same time as the galaxy they're in.

There are other types. **Stealth** black holes take in material at a slower rate. Stealth means secret. Black holes can also be sorted by several properties or traits, including **rotations**. Rotations are turns or spins.

DOWN-TO-EARTH EXPERIMENT

Want to learn more about the universe and black holes? Try out this experiment.

Learn how pressure and gravity work. Think like a space scientist!

Materials:

- Balloon
- Aluminum foil sheets
- Pin

Instructions:

1. Blow up the balloon. Tie it closed. The balloon represents a star's hot burning core.

2. Wrap the balloon in several layers of foil. The layers represent the star's different gas layers. A star's core heat puts pressure on the gas layers. This keeps the star from collapsing.

3. Lightly press on the balloon covered in foil with your hands. You'll feel resistance. This is how gravity and stars work. Your hands represent the force of gravity. The star exists because the gravity and the star's core pressure balance each other out.

4. Pop the balloon using the pin. (Don't crush the shape of the foil!) This represents a star at the end of its life. The star's core runs out of fuel. There's no more pressure. It's no longer able to hold up the gas layers.

5. Gravity still exists. Squeeze the foil into a ball. You'll notice there is resistance. There's a lot of pressure. This is how black holes are formed. The mass of the small ball is the same as that of the model star. But their sizes are different.

CHAPTER THREE

WHAT DO BLACK HOLES DO?

Black holes pull in things. They eat everything in their way. But they're not hungry **predators**. Predators are hunters. Black holes don't hunt planets. They don't hunt stars. They pull things that **orbit** close to them. Orbit means to circle around.

Black holes also spit things out. They fling out spitballs. These spitballs travel up to 20 million miles (32 million kilometers) per hour. They're the size of planets. They're made of gas, dust, and matter. These planet-sized spitballs travel so fast that they end up in another galaxy.

One day, starships might travel between solar systems. These machines haven't been invented yet.

Gravity is strongest at a black hole's center. It **warps** space and time. Warp means to twist or bend. Laws of science no longer exist in the center. The black hole's center is known as singularity. Singularity is a place of **infinitely** dense matter. Infinite means having no limits. This singularity slows down time.

If you could stand outside the black hole, you would feel time slowing down. As you moved closer to the singularity, you'd be pulled in. Time would slow down even more. Time is affected by how fast people travel. People on Earth would experience normal time.

As you moved toward singularity, you'd be stretched out. You'd be "**spaghettified**." This means being stretched out like a spaghetti noodle.

A person who travels through space is younger than a person who stays on Earth. The faster one moves, the slower time passes.

IT'S (ALMOST) ROCKET SCIENCE

LIGO is the Laser Interferometer Gravitational-Wave Observatory. It's the world's largest observatory. It studies light and space. It seeks to find and understand gravitational waves. It listens for the waves. It feels the waves. It studies black holes. It looks at 2 black holes merging. Merging means joining. As black holes merge, they emit gravitational waves. LIGO studies these waves. LIGO is special. First, it's blind. It doesn't see electromagnetic radiation. Radiation means energy that comes from a source. This energy takes the form of waves or rays. This comes from things like light and radio. LIGO is isolated from the outside world. This lets it focus only on gravitational waves. Second, LIGO is not round. Its machines are L-shaped. It doesn't need to collect light from stars. So, it doesn't need to have round lenses like telescopes. Third, LIGO can't make a discovery on its own. It needs 2 machines. Each machine verifies the other one. The machines are 1,865 miles (3,001 km) apart. They're in remote areas in Washington and Louisiana.

CHAPTER FOUR

ARE BLACK HOLES DANGEROUS?

The forces of black holes are like strong storm waves. These waves pull things in. They pull toward the singularity. The singularity rips things apart. It destroys things. Things disappear before reaching singularity. They stop existing. In this way, black holes are dangerous.

 Wormholes are tiny tears in space-time.

Scientists don't think anything could escape from black holes. But they have theories about **wormholes**. Wormholes are tunnels. They go through space and time. They connect one black hole to another. Some people think wormholes are ways to travel from one galaxy to another. But there's no proof of wormholes.

Black holes are scary. They're destructive. They're final. But don't worry. Earth won't fall into a black hole. No black hole is close enough to Earth's solar system. It's unlikely the Sun would become a black hole. It's not big enough.

If the Sun does become a black hole, Earth would still not fall in. The black hole would have the same mass as the Sun. Earth and the other planets would orbit the black hole. They'd orbit in the same way they do now.

 Earth isn't on a collision course with any known black holes.

21

CHAPTER → FIVE

DO BLACK HOLES DIE?

At first, scientists thought black holes lived forever. But nothing in the universe lives forever.

There's a new theory about the lives of black holes. Black holes emit radiation. Black hole radiation carries away energy. In this way, black holes would lose energy. They'd shrink.

They'd **evaporate** into nothing. Evaporate means to turn water into gas. Everything inside the black holes would disappear as well. This process would take billions of years.

 Black holes won't be dying anytime soon.

There's another theory. Black holes would hit a point. This is a point where they can't collapse any more. There'd be nothing left to close in. This means black holes would stop existing. They'd explode. They'd become white holes. They'd spit out everything. They'd bounce. White holes wouldn't let anything in. This process would happen quickly. It'd happen in less than a second. This is just an idea. There's no proof of white holes. Scientists see **flares** in the galaxy. Flares are bursts of fire. These flares may be the last bits of black holes.

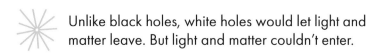 Unlike black holes, white holes would let light and matter leave. But light and matter couldn't enter.

25

CHAPTER SIX

WHO FIRST STUDIED BLACK HOLES?

Dr. Albert Einstein lived from 1879 to 1955. He studied **physics**. Physics is the science of matter and energy. Einstein is thought to be one of the greatest minds. He first predicted black holes in 1916. He came up with a theory. He inspired people to think about space and time.

 Schwarzschild took pictures of stars.

Dr. Karl Schwarzschild lived from 1873 to 1916. He built on Einstein's work. He discovered black holes. He developed the modern idea of black holes. Modern means current.

Dr. John Wheeler lived from 1911 to 2008. He came up with the term "black hole."

Dr. Stephen Hawking lived from 1942 to 2018. He was an English physicist. He studied the **origin** and evolution of the universe. Origin means beginning.

Hawking was a world-famous scientist. He studied black holes. He provided math **equations** that proved black holes were real. Equations are math statements. Scientists use equations to explain things. Hawking was the first to say that black holes would evaporate away. Black hole radiation is called Hawking radiation.

Hawking studied black holes even when others didn't believe. He said, "Look up at the stars and not down at your feet. Try to make sense of what you see. And wonder about what makes the universe exist. Be curious."

 Hawking radiation can't be seen in space. But it can be studied in science labs.

29

DENSE (DENS) crowded and packed in, solid

EQUATIONS (ih-KWAY-zhuhnz) mathematical statements used to explain how things are equal

EVAPORATE (ih-VAP-uh-rate) to turn liquid into gas

FLARES (FLAIRZ) bursts of light

GRAVITY (GRAV-ih-tee) force that attracts things to fall toward Earth's center

INFINITELY (IN-fuh-nit-lee) without an end or limits

INTERMEDIATE (in-tur-MEE-dee-it) coming between things

MASS (MAS) the amount of matter in an object

ORBIT (OR-bit) to circle around

ORIGIN (OR-ih-jin) the beginning

PHYSICS (FIZ-iks) science of matter and energy

PREDATORS (PRED-uh-turz) hunters

PRIMORDIAL (pry-MOR-dee-uhl) existing at the beginning of time

ROTATIONS (roh-TAY-shuhnz) spins or turns

SOLAR (SOH-lur) relating to the sun

SPAGHETTIFIED (spuh-GET-ee-fide) to be stretched out like a spaghetti noodle

STEALTH (STELTH) secret, sneaky

THEORY (THEER-ee) an idea meant to explain something

WARPS (WORPS) distorts, twists, or bends

WORMHOLES (WURM-holez) tunnels through space and time that connect one black hole to another

FAR-OUT FACTS

- There are many films and movies about black holes. In *Interstellar* (2014), characters travel through a wormhole. They enter a black hole. In *Star Trek* (2009), the villain creates a black hole in order to destroy a planet.

- The Milky Way has its own black hole. The black hole is called Sagittarius A. It's a supermassive black hole. It has the mass of 4 million suns. It's about 26,000 light-years away from Earth. A light-year is the distance that light travels in 1 year. It was discovered in 1838.

- There are scientists in South Africa. They discovered a special place in space. They're calling it ELAIS-N1. They found supermassive black holes in several galaxies spinning in the same direction. This is odd. They're 300 million light-years apart. The scientists are using the Giant Metrewave Radio Telescope in India. They want to learn more about the origins of the universe.

LEARN MORE

DeCristofano, Carolyn Cinami, and Michael Carroll (illustr.). *A Black Hole Is Not a Hole.* Watertown, MA: Charlesbridge, 2017.

Kurtz, Kevin. *Black Holes in Action.* Minneapolis, MN: Lerner Publications, 2020.

Tyson, Neil deGrasse, with Gregory Mone. *Astrophysics for Young People in a Hurry.* New York, NY: Norton Young Readers, 2019.

INDEX

"big bang," 4–5, 10
black holes
   danger from, 18–21
   death of, 22–25
   types of, 10–13
   what they are, 6–9
   what they do, 14–17
Bouman, Katie, 9

Cygnus X-1, 7

dust, 4, 8, 14

Einstein, Albert, 26
"event horizon," 8
Event Horizon
   Telescope, 9
experiment, 13

galaxies, 4, 12, 31
gases, 4, 8, 14, 23
gravitational waves, 17
gravity, 6, 8, 10, 13, 15

Hawking, Stephen, 28

intermediate black
   holes, 11, 12

light, 6, 17, 24
LIGO (Laser Interferometer
   Gravitational-Wave
   Observatory), 17

mass, 10, 11, 12
matter, 4, 5, 8, 10,
   14, 15, 24
Milky Way, 4, 5, 11, 31

pressure, 13
primordial black holes,
   10

radiation, 17, 22, 28

Schwarzschild, Karl, 27
singularity, 15–16, 18
solar systems, 4
spitballs, 14
stars, 7, 8, 10, 12
stealth black holes, 12
stellar black holes, 10
sun, 11, 12, 20
supermassive black
   holes, 9, 11, 12, 31

telescopes, 7, 9, 31
time warp, 15–16

universe, 4–5, 28

Wheeler, John, 27
white holes, 24
women, 9
wormholes, 19

ABOUT THE AUTHOR

Dr. Virginia Loh-Hagan is an author, university professor, and former classroom teacher. She likes using black holes in metaphors. For example, when she writes, she enters a black hole. She lives in San Diego, California, with her very tall husband and very naughty dogs. To learn more about her, visit www.virginialoh.com.